SHEROES
of the
Haitian Revolution

Written by
Bayyinah Bello

Illustrated by
Kervin Andre

Dedicated

To my mother Marie Christine Marie Louise Domerson, this warrior, who made it a daily mission to move heaven and earth to provide the needs of her siblings, her children, grandchildren, and neighbors. What a force of nature!

"Know thyself, all the way to your Createss, and this Truth shall make you free."

-Bayyinah Bello

Author's Note

History or 'his story' is the story of the men existing on a land within a parenthesis of time. Ourstory captures the light from the stories created by the mingling of relations, decisions, vibrations, actions, inspirations... of Ancestors, Elders, women, men, young and old, newborn and centenarians, as well as plants and animals, elements and climatic behaviors existing on a particular space/time. Guided by the spirit of our Ancestors, under the protection of the Divine Mother, this servant of the People wishes to share a bit of the ourstory of Ayiti (free from the imposed Eurochristian vision of what happened), with an emphasis on the contribution of women. Women, the expression of the primordial energies! Women, who have been so systematically left out in all of the 'his story' books of the world! That is not feminism, that is justice!

Ayiti is the land of the Arawak People. This particular island bore the name Ayiti for over four thousand years prior to its invasion by Eurochristian thieves and criminals. In those days, the island bore three names: Ayiti, Kiskeya and Boyo. Twelve ethnic groups and a group of Afrikans, mainly from Egypt, Phoenicia and Mali shared it. The most recent ones came with the expedition of the Malian (king), Mansa Abu Bakari II, brother of his successor to the Malian throne, Mansa Musa, in 1311.

That was before so-called Africa and America suffered the barbarous system of slavery established by Eurochristians on these continents. Eurochristian slavery made it legal to practice genocide against the non-white peoples of the world, to kidnap Afrikans and bring them anywhere, and to America in particular. America, with its forged laws and practices dictated by greed and inhumanity that forced Afrikans to become something other than themselves, slaves. Therefore, Ayiti's ourstory began simultaneously here with the Arawaks over 4,000 years ago and there with the Afrikans, more than 10,000 years ago. In fact, in an attempt to approach correctness, we should use a term like Khemitians instead of Africans. Hope you meet yourself as you read the various bios offered in this book.

Anakaona
Kasikess

Anakaona was a Kasikess (queen) born into the royal court of the kingdom of Ayiti. Early on, she exhibited many talents appreciated in her community. She shone with spiritual powers, intelligence, great oratory skills, and an ability to inspire trust in the People. She was a fine singer, poet, and sports person, too. Already as a young girl, she was often called to assist her older brother Bohekio at the head of the Xaragwa Kasika. The position naturally became hers after Bohekio's removal, due to illness. Anakaona sat as an equal among the five "Kasiks," forming the crown that governed the entire island of Ayiti/Kiskeya/Boyo. She was married to the intrepid Kaonabo who was Kasik of Magwana.

In the year 1492, Eurochristians savagely invaded Ayiti, and with lies and scams, slaughtered the four male members of the crown within three years. Anakaona was now the only living member of the crown. Through her extraordinary talents and statewomanship, she was not only able to survive but to lead the fight against the vicious invaders. She mounted armies of thousands, armed with bows and arrows, to confront the heavily armed enemy. Under her leadership, they won many battles.

Due to the success of Kasikess Anakaona's resistance, the Spanish crown sent in a new Governor to attempt to crush her defense. The ruthless Ovando sent a peace offering to which Anakaona eventually agreed. It ended up being a trap, and Anakaona was captured. She was tried, found guilty of treason against Spain, and sentenced to death. She was offered clemency if she would convert to Catholicism and agree to be a concubine to one of the European officers. She refused. Kasikess Anakaona was then hanged and burned at the stake on October 3, 1503.

Anakaona's legacy lived on in her nephew, Kasik Henry, who led one of the most successful resistance efforts in new generation Tayno history. Henry's revolt resulted in the first treaty signed in the Americas by Indigenous people with Eurochristians. Kasikess Anakaona's story continues to inspire millions of women and men to pursue the fight against injustice in the collective interest.

Cecile Fatimah

Organization Expert

Cecile Fatimah was one of the most highly respected, sought after mambo in the French slave colony of Saint Domingue. Born in France to a Senegalese mother and a white French father, she was the oldest of two girls and one boy. No one knows why her Corsican father abruptly sold his wife and children into slavery. Upon arriving in Saint Domingue, she never saw her family again. She quickly made a name for herself on the plantation with her striking beauty and vivid green eyes. Usually a woman with features as attractive as Cecile's would be confined to house slave status; however, her un-submissiveness relegated her to field work.

As a captive assigned to field work, she grew into a Master of Communication and formed codified networks all over the island. It was at this point that she began to organize what would eventually become the only successful revolt of Afrikan captives in ourstory. Cecile trained her network to be stealth while transmitting information from plantation to plantation, miles away from each other. She created codes for names of places and people so that enslaved informants could not notify slavers. It took Cecile and her network of women years to organize the most famous gathering in Haitian ourstory, now referred to in books as the ceremony at Bwa Kayiman. Participants in this long-awaited congress of the savagely chained Afrikan captives, included some freed women and men, as well as some maroons. Each had their own ideas on how the fight for freedom could be won. Some didn't believe that freedom was possible at all. That is precisely when the Afrikan captive Bookman, a coachman, rose from his position and delivered a speech now referred to as Bookman's prayer. This text resonates throughout ourstory. With everyone in agreement on how to move forward, Cecile then presided over the ceremony during which everyone attending took the sacred oath, freedom or death. Thirteen years after the Bwa Kayiman ceremony, freedom was won.

Cecile lived to celebrate and enjoy independence and many years after that. Eventually, a clear minded Cecile transitioned to the Ancestors' realm at the ripe old age of 112.

Aunt Tòya

Agbaraya

Agbaraya Tòya was a well-respected, highly accomplished warrior for the Empire of Dahomey in Africa. She had reached the military position of gaou (general) in the all-female army under the then king of Dahomey, Dada Tegbessou, whose personal security she assured.

Around the year 1753, Tòya's village was raided by Eurochristian slavers. After a remarkable fight, Tòya was able to disarm and defeat a number of the pale men. She eventually was captured into a net and brought to the slave ships docked at the shore, awaiting their horrified cargo. After the long journey from Dahomey to Saint Domingue, Aunt Tòya was ushered onto the auction block where, after numerous humiliations, she was purchased by a slaver. Soon after arriving on the slaver's plantation, Tòya escaped and headed straight to the mountains. For many days and nights she attempted to recruit other maroons to join her army, but she didn't meet the right people. Ultimately, she befriended a runaway woman who was about to deliver a baby. Tòya stopped to help her. The new mother insisted that Tòya take possession of the newborn boy and teach him freedom. She agreed. Tòya made the decision to return to the plantation with the child in order to effectively train him in the ways of Dahomey. She taught him the Yoruba language, the art and science of war, and a take-no-prisoners approach to battle. Tòya and the boy were continually separated by their slavers; however, divine nature would each time make their paths cross again. The boy would grow up to be the first leader of independent Hayti. Now meet the military marvel: Jean-Jacques Dessalines.

After the French were defeated and freedom won, Dessalines became Emperor of Hayti and Tòya was reunited with her protégé once again. The reunion was short lived as Tòya fell terminally ill. Dessalines issued his best doctors to her bedside, but ultimately on June 12, 1805, Agbaraya Tòya transitioned to join the ancestors' realm. Emperor Jacques mobilized his military to offer to Agbaraya Tòya the simplest and most dignified state funeral in the history of the Free Black Empire.

Sanite Bélair

Lieutenant

Lieutenant Sanite Bélair was an officer in the revolutionary army of Saint Domingue. Born and raised in the town of Verrettes, Sanite was always a very brave girl and loved to compete and win against her older brothers.

When Sanite turned 16 years old, she married Colonel Charles Bélair, who had fallen madly in love with her. Shortly thereafter, Sanite joined the revolutionary army. Sanite seemed to be born for military service and quickly reached the rank of lieutenant.

In the year 1801, Napoleon Bonaparte, now the dictator of France, sent an expedition of over 20,000 soldiers to re-enslave the black population of Saint Domingue. Sanite quickly became a target, and a price was placed on her head...Dead or Alive. Being the brave, un-intimidated woman that she was, Sanite refused to go into hiding at first. She finally yielded to family pressure due to the fact that she was again with child.

Sanite was eventually captured by French Colonel Repussard. When General Charles Bélair learned of his wife's capture, he turned himself in to French authorities, requesting they take him instead of his wife. They were both arrested, found guilty of conspiracy, and sentenced for execution.

On October 5, 1802 in Cap Francais, Sanite and Charles Bélair were brought out by the French for execution. Charles was given the standard execution for a military officer, death by firing squad. As she looked at her husband, she encouraged him to die bravely. Sanite was to be executed by decapitation, which was reserved for women. As the French executioners attempted to place her head on the guillotine, Sanite fought them off. Ultimately, Sanite refused any blindfold and ordered the firing squad to take position, aim, and fire upon her. It would be the final command she gave.

The legacy of Lieutenant Sanite Bélair continues to inspire future generations of revolutionary women.

Marie-Jeanne

Director of Spy Office and Sharp Shooter

Marie-Jeanne was a maroon and an extraordinary spy from Port Republican, now known as Port-au-Prince. She refused to be called mulatto, preferring the term "mixed blood" that acknowledged her dominant inheritance of Afrikan and Arawak blood. She was tall, slender, highly muscular, and a master at the art of disguise.

During the war of independence, the most common warrior bands were made up of men, women, and children. The rarest were constituted exclusively of women, such as the one directed by Marie-Jeanne. She always took her responsibilities very seriously. When General Louis-Daure Lamartinière, asked her to marry him, she responded: "Let's build our country first and our home later."

No one can mention The Battle of Crête-a-Pierrot, a turning point in Haiti's war for independence, without referring to the extraordinary accomplishments of Marie-Jeanne. On March 2, 1802, nearly 600 revolutionaries were at the old fort of Crête-a-Pierrot to take measurements for eventual repairs. Suddenly, they found themselves besieged by 12,000 French soldiers. The French were certain it would take less than an hour to kill everyone and take the fort.

Despite having neither food nor water, and running out of ammunition and weapons, our women and men continued to fight daily and inflicted great damages on the French army's ranks.

On March 22, General Lamartinière sent a note of despair to General Dessalines. He showed it to Marie-Jeanne who responded with a plan that the two of them sneak into the Fort to build-up the morale of the troops. In that fort, Dessalines swore that he would lead them to independence.

Marie-Jeanne returned to the fort with some of her female warriors, dressed in a mamlouk outfit and toting a shotgun in one hand and a dagger in the other. While fighting they motivated our troops to keep the stones and sticks striking the enemy. Many accounts have Marie-Jeanne standing on the walls of the fort exhibiting incredible war feats. Finally, she conceived a brilliant military maneuver by which the troops, like lighting, dashed out of the fort to cross the French troops, and more than 350 Ayitian soldiers came through alive.

Ultimately, Marie-Jeanne became the head of the Imperial Spy and Security Office.

Marie-Jeanne is a prime example of feminine brilliance, courage, determination, and proof that those who invest their efforts can accomplish what they will. When looking for a leading example of the stock Ayitian women are made of, don't hesitate to look in the direction of Marie-Jeanne.

Suzanne Simon Louverture

Expert Farmer

Suzanne Simon was partner, caretaker, and wife of one of the most powerful men in ourstory, Toussaint Louverture.

Suzanne Simon chose not to participate in her husband's public life. She concentrated on making sure that the harvest was plentiful on her farms. She took pleasure in welcoming those who visited her home, serving them foods agreeable to their tastes, and making sure her table could feed all who came to her home.

On June 7, 1802, the French army descended upon General Louverture's home and arrested Suzanne Simon, their sons, and many others that Suzanne cared for in the Louverture household. Being the composed woman that she was, there were no cries, no supplications, no accusations, and no blaming. She was not allowed to take any spare clothing, neither for her nor for any other family member.

On the boat to France, Suzanne ran into her husband just once. Before the guards could do anything, she jumped into his arms and placed some money from her bosom into his pocket, grabbing a last kiss from her beloved before the guards savagely pulled her away from him. Convinced that Toussaint who was a great general, wouldn't buckle under his torturing methods, Napoleon ordered that they impose on Suzanne all the tortures they would have liked to inflict on Toussaint. Upon entering the jailhouse in Agens, Suzanne was brutally tortured for months in an attempt to force her to reveal the whereabouts of her husband's presumed fortunes. She persisted with a single reply: "I won't speak about my husband to his torturers."

As much as the oral and written accounts concerning her life concur, the information about her death diverges. Once released by the British authorities who were then occupying France, she received a pension of 150 francs per month. Some report that she died of cancer in 1816 at the age of 80; others that she transitioned in Jamaica.

Prior to the fight for freedom, Suzanne and Toussaint were practically inseparable as Toussaint wrote in a letter *"Until the moment of the revolution, I had not left my wife for an hour."*

Kerin"

Katherine Flon
Entrepreneur

Katherine Flon was a very talented seamstress who owned a cloth store in the town of Arcahaie. Her light skin didn't stop her great heart from getting involved in the fight for freedom.

After a battle in February 1802, General Dessalines intentionally ripped the white stripe off the French tricolor flag to demonstrate to French General Brunet his determination to sever all ties with French colonial domination. On the spot, he ordered General Clerveau to form the commission that would create the flag of our nation. Ms. Katherine Flon was recommended to General Clerveau by the healer and mambo Grann Guiton.

Katherine was already very much involved in the fight for independence. Once the slave revolts started in 1791, her whole family fled the colony to find refuge elsewhere. Katherine, single and still in her twenties, decided to stay and contribute in any way she could. Eventually, she was nursing the sick and wounded after nearby battles. When Katherine was officially commissioned by Dessalines to create the new national flag, she wasted no time putting together a committee to brainstorm different colors that would best represent the spirit of a people who had accomplished such exploits in their fight for freedom. The committee, headed by Katherine, eventually decided to have a black and red vertical flag: black representing the people and red representing victory as well as its cost. Katherine and her team also established parameters for how the flag should be handled, folded, stored, and saluted.

Katherine and her team of seamstresses had sewed official national flags of various dimensions for different official buildings, and they were placed on numerous establishments all across the Free Black Empire.

Katherine Flon is a woman to whom the Ayitian nation owes much. In the year 2000, the Haitian government placed an image of a woman sewing a flag on a 10-gourde note to celebrate Katherine's contributions to the nation's independence.

Marissainte Dedee Bazile

Head of Logistics

Marissainte Dedee Bazile was a valuable contributor to the Haitian revolution. She was born to Afrikan parents into the ferocious slavery system of Saint Domingue. She grew up in Cap-Haitian, married a goldsmith, and had two children at a young age. The whole family began following military troops and providing them with various services: blacksmithing, laundering, cooking, and finding supplies.

History books usually refer to her as "Defilez Lafolle," meaning "March on Crazy Woman," but this moniker is a grave injustice to a shero who contributed generously to the fight for independence. Ultimately, she joined the camp of General Dessalines and quickly climbed the ranks, eventually being named Head of Supplies. Marissainte Dedee Bazile enjoyed the reputation of being a fair and impartial woman. When meals were prepared for the camp, she was known to serve soldiers before officers. She lost siblings, children, and a husband on the battlefields, like so many others during that period.

She is most affectionately referred to as Dedee and is remembered primarily for her actions after the assassination of Haiti's first chief of state, Emperor Jacques. After the ambush, then the killing, the Emperor's body was dismembered and scattered about Port-au-Prince. Once Dedee heard about the death of the Emperor, she made her plan. She raced to the scene, and in a brave and determined effort, she gathered the body parts of the Emperor with the aid of Placide Dauphin. They ensured he had an honorable burial at the Principal Cemetery of Port-au-Prince. The woman who is often called "crazy" defied official declarations and threats to bury the man who brought independence to Hayti. Dedee passed away in the year 1816. Her surviving son lived to become a colonel in the military of Haiti's second Empire led by Emperor Faustin 1st.

Marie-Louise

Queen of Hayti

Marie-Louise Coidavid was the first and only Queen in the history of independent Haiti. Born on May 8, 1778 to a free black family in the commune of Ouanaminthe, Marie-Louise flourished into an intelligent, poised, and gifted young lady according to the colonial norms of the time. Marie-Louise had just turned sixteen when she married the future king of Hayti, Christophe Henry, on July 15, 1793. The union of Marie-Louise Coidavid and Christophe Henry produced four children: François-Ferdinand (May 15, 1794); Françoise-Amethyst born on May 9, 1798; Anne-Athénaïse born on July 7, 1800; and Jacques-Victor born on March 3, 1804.

Christophe's extraordinary talents caused him to rapidly move up the ranks in Toussaint Louverture's army. He soon attained the rank of General, controlling most of the northern army. After the assassination of Jean-Jacques Dessalines, Hayti was divided into the Republic of Haiti in the West/South and the Kingdom of Hayti in the North. Marie-Louise and Christophe were crowned on June 2, 1811. At thirty-three years of age, she became Queen Marie-Louise of Hayti.

Marie-Louise had to play the role of an officer's wife, weathering the sleeplessness of moving from camp to camp and from castle to forest. At times, she experienced some of the best the world could offer, but at other times she endured some of the worst. She lived through the assassination of her first born in France, and she buried her husband and all her children. She was placed under house arrest and then forced into exile in Europe.

Eventually, she settled in Pisa, Italy. Though isolated and overwhelmed by a destiny that had brought her ruin, Queen Marie-Louise always kept her chin up in the face of adversity. She appealed to her sister, Madame Louise Pierrot, who obtained permission to join her in Italy. And it was in her sister's arms that she died in Pisa at the age of 73, on March 14, 1851. She and her two daughters rested in the same cemetery, at least until 1966, when the author of these biographies had the honor of visiting their graves and showering them with candles, perfumes and flowers.

Felicite

Empress of Hayti

Marie Claire Heureuse Felicite Bonheur was born into slavery, and rose to become not only a free woman, educator, natural healer, and war nurse, but also a constitutionalist, author, adoptive mother to dozens of children, and eventually, the first Empress of Hayti, Empire of Freedom.

Felicite was born in Leogane on May 8, 1748. Although she was enslaved as a youth, she managed to learn to read and write the French language. A very beautiful woman, Felicite was purchased by the French painter, Michel Petit, whom she would eventually marry. As a gift to his new bride, Michel Petit bought her mother and father out of slavery. He died five years later.

As a young widow, Felicite enjoyed a good reputation as an educator, teaching many free Blacks how to read and write. Soon she very successfully assumed the role of treating wounds and ailments with plants. It was while using her skills as an herbalist and healer on a battlefield near Gonaives that she ran into Colonel Jean-Jacques Dessalines. On April 2, 1800, they wedded at the cathedral in Saint Marc.

On October 8, 1804, General Dessalines was crowned Jacques, Emperor 1st of Hayti, Empire of Freedom, and his wife was crowned Empress Felicite. As Empress, little changed in her practice of sharing and service to all. Empress Felicite actively participated in the writing of the Imperial Constitution of 1805, including clauses to help protect children and to promote the reuniting of black families torn apart under slavery.

On October 17, 1806, an evil plot carried out by enemies of Dessalines ended his life and made Empress Felicite a widow again. She would live out the rest of her life modestly, still pursuing her life's mission of serving the underprivileged, even when she herself was barely surviving. This wonderful soul departed on August 8, 1858, at the age of 110.

Empress Felicite is responsible for one of Haiti's most cherished traditions, celebrating freedom with a generous distribution of Independence Soup (Soup Joumou) which she served from January 1-7 yearly throughout the country. In this manner she sought to ensure that the nation celebrated freedom in solidarity and without hunger.

Words from our Sheroes

Queen Marie-Louise on the day she was crowned:

"Gentlemen,

The name of Queen that the nation has just bestowed on me binds me even more particularly to the plight of the Haitian people, for which I have always glorified myself to be a tender mother.

I will not forget on the throne the duties imposed by the Royal Majesty, and when my family is destined to take place, it is enough to enlighten me about the extreme care that I must bring to her upbringing. Yes, my children will be my most expensive adornment, since on them must one day depend the destiny of my homeland."

"Gonaïves, November 11th, 1804

Wife Henry Christophe to her dear husband, It is with real pleasure, my dear and good friend, that I take this favorable opportunity to let you know that we all are enjoying perfect health, except however, for Victor who is a little inconvenienced, I think it is, beause he is teething. I like to believe that it's nothing. I have been deprived of your dear news for a few days; If you knew the satisfaction I feel when I receive it, you would give it to me every day. I beg you to press the laundress for my laundry, because I and my children are on the eve of lacking clothes. You know how hard it is to get the clothing bleached around here. When it's ready, order them to bring it to me right away. The sugar that you have announced to me has not arrived yet. This delay disrupts us a bit, because we look forward to it. Especially, Mrs Dessalines who was hoping to teach me how to make ice cream based on your promise to send us sugar. She and her ladies send their compliments to you.

Our children join me in wishing you good health and we embrace you from the depths of our soul.

Your affectionate wife,

Spouse of H. Christophe"

Words from our Sheroes

Letter of Empress Felicite to General Etienne Gerin, named Minister of War and Sea

"Général,

On pouvait croire que vous alliez, après le crime odieux au Pont Rouge, vous faire oublier, mais au contraire, vous allez, dans votre folie vengeresse, jusqu'à menacer la femme d'un homme, lequel, après tout, n'a fait que du bien pour ce pays que vous prétendez relever. J'ai noté avec autant de satisfaction que vous méritez de mépris les injures dont vous accablez mon mari, après l'avoir si lâchement assassiné. Je ne voulais pas répondre à vos attaques stupides, mais c'en est trop, je tenais à vous faire comprendre que vous n'êtes qu'un vulgaire assassin, dussé-je mourir moi aussi par vos coups. Recevez mes civilités empressées. "

"General,

One might have thought, after the heinous crime at Pont Rouge, that you were going to allow people to forget about you; but on the contrary, you go, in your vengeful madness, to the point of threatening the wife of a man, who, after all, has done nothing but good for this country that you claim to want to take to a higher level. I have noted with much satisfaction that you deserve contempt for the insults which you are overwhelmingly lobbing on my late husband, after having so cowardly murdered him. I did not want to respond to your stupid attacks, but enough is enough, I only want to make sure you know, that you are nothing but a vulgar murderer, even if I, too, must die by your blows.

Eagerly, receive my civilities. "

"No one could appreciate freedom while hunger thunders in his belly. If there is one among us with no food, the rest of the citizens cannot celebrate freedom on the Earth. In order for your celebration to be true, those who have plenty must harness the responsibility to share with those who have less." -Empress Felicite

Bio
Bayyinah Bello

Born on Thursday, March 25th, 1948, Bayyinah is the eldest of seven sisters, the mother of three sons: Hashim-Thawab, Siddiq Theo-dile, Yahya Akil and a daughter: Ameerah Anakaona. She is a grandmother of nine: five girls and four boys and great-grandma of four. Spouse of deep African thoughts and lover of Ayiti's ourstory, Bayyinah Bello discovered her commitment to education before the age of 10 and was introduced to this field through literacy programs in Nigeria. Once she had completed her primary education in Haiti, she was sent to Liberia to live with her mother. After completing her classical studies in France, she joined her mother in New York. In this city, she earned a college degree in education. Back in Africa, she obtained a Masters in linguistics, diplomas and certificates in interpreting... Her professional career began in 1969, in the United States of America. She discovered the joys of writing in 1970, with the birth of her first-born for whom she wrote her first children's stories. In Nigeria, she uncovered her passion for history and the Arabic language, which allowed her to explore other literary and historical perceptions. Back in the USA, she worked as a publicist at the Museum of Natural History. In Ayiti, taught at the State University and founded a primary and secondary bilingual school, Citadelle International School. In Togo, she taught English and Arabic in different financial institutions. Today, her energies are concentrated in building the "Marie Claire Heureuse Félicité Bonheur Dessalines Foundation" also called "FONDASYON FELICITEE" (FF) for historical research and identity, whose ultimate goal is to establish an "Ayitian" educational system aiming to build a conscientious "Ayitian," aware of her/his strength, because they know their cultural vision, work with tools of their own, confident in their abilities to bring about better conditions of living for all.

Bio
Kervin Andre

Kervin A. Andre is a visual artist whose proud Haitian Heritage emanates from every brushstroke. He was born and raised in Port-Au-Prince, Haiti. Kervin's talent was birthed amidst the beauty and splendor of the First Black Republic in the Americas. Throughout the years, this self-taught artist, has honed his skills and exercises his artistic talents through many mediums. Kervin's spent his formative years in Haiti and move to Elizabeth NJ at the age of 15 with his family. It is these years that have shaped his deep appreciation for his culture and it's rich history. He started drawing at an early age, but it was not until his 20s when he attended an art event that he realized he could turn his passion into a career. Kervin is the beloved father of two beautiful daughters, who motivate him daily. He is committed to leaving a legacy behind for his daughters and others. He wants to instill a sense of pride, heritage, culture and true knowledge of self. His artwork displays an acute sense of pride and social responsibility. He credits his intellectual curiosity to his father and his strength and resilience to his mother. All of his subjects depict strength, resilience and hope. Kervin spends countless amount of time researching his subjects as he dives into each piece. He draws inspiration from everything around him. All of Kervin's art is focused on uplifting and realizing the power of who we are as a people. "My art is a testament of the social injustices going on in the world today, especially those affecting the Black community."

www.akomicsart.com

kervin.andre@yahoo.com

Instagram: @akomicsart

Facebook: http://facebook.com/akomicsart

Bio
Thorobred Books

Frantz Derenoncourt, Jr. is a first generation Haitian-American born and raised in Brooklyn, NY. After very humble beginnings he attended Virginia State University in Petersburg, VA where he majored in Business Management and soon after moved to the nations capitol, Washington, DC. After working a few 9 to 5 jobs around town, Frantz fell in love with the real estate industry and found success as a real estate sales professional and real estate investor. As a child growing up in Brooklyn in the early 80s, Frantz was often picked on for being Haitian. Teachers could never pronounce his name correctly and the students would always have a cruel Haitian joke on hand. At times, he felt ashamed to be Haitian until he started reading about Haitian history. The fact that his little country accomplished something that no other nation had gave him a tremendous sense of pride. He started reading everything he could get his hands on in regards to the Haitian Revolution and relaying the stories to his own children. When he saw that his kids were just as excited as he was, Frantz then realized that these fascinating stories needed to be told in a way that even elementary age children could appreciate the accomplishment of their ancestors. Thus, Thorobred Books was born.

Mission Statement

My mission for Thorobred Books is to establish a sense of pride in the black youth all over the world. I also aim to tell the stories of success and victory when we come together as a people against impossible odds. I also publish to let the world know that if you're a person of color from Haiti, Dominican Republic, Cuba, the United States or any other nation, all of our ancestors came from the same place. A win for one of us, is a win for all of us.

Keep In Contact with
Bayyinah Bello
and
FONDASYON FÉLICITÉE

FONDASYON FÉLICITÉE
Village Théodat Rue À #4
Tabarre, Haïti 6124
(509) 22 48 22 38
www.fondasyonfelicitee.com
Email: bayyinahbello@fondasyonfelicitee.com
Instagram: @fondasyon_felicitee
Instagram: @bayyinahbello
Facebook: Bayyinah E. Bello

Also from
Thorobred Books

Get the whole
Haitian Heroes
Collection
at
www.thorobredbook.com